The
Black Book
For
Entrepreneurs

Copyright section:

Copyright 2010 By Robert D. Pettiford

Library of Congress Cataloging-in-Publication Data

Pettiford, Robert D.

Library of Congress Control Number: 2010913351

The Black Book for Entrepreneurs

ISBN-10 0615410588

ISBN-13 9780615410586

About the book

"The Black Book for Entrepreneurs" is a combination of a motivational/inspirational and a how-to book. It is not just written for entrepreneurs; it is written for anyone that wishes to follow his/her dreams and make those dreams a reality.

❧

This book is dedicated to my children Roel, Robert, and Michael Pettiford. They have all taught me more about life and being a good person than anyone else. They have all shown me that the entrepreneurial and leadership spirit can and is passed down.

❧

Acknowledgments

Thank you to everyone in my support groups, especially Rita Pettiford, Nisha Mathson, and Deon A. Brown for taking time out of your busy schedules and assisting with the editing. Brenda M. Dainton and Lauren Wilson for assistance with the layout of the book and Tinay A. Sevilla, photographer. Thank you, Sifu Dan Anderson of Anderson Martial Arts in New York City, N.Y. who was responsible for teaching me to capture every opportunity. And a special thank you to all of the entrepreneurs out there still grinding. Keep grinding. I am with you.

Contents

Introduction

The purpose of this book is to assist entrepreneurs, leaders, and start-ups in several different aspects. It focuses on the business with motivational and leadership undertones. I decided to write this book as a result of people coming to me and asking for my assistance with business planning and consulting. I found that there are great books to assist entrepreneurs out there, but a lot of them are long and not straight to the point.

I wanted entrepreneurs to know how, when, where, and at what time one should open a business. I also wanted entrepreneurs to know they are not alone in their business ideas, their vision, and most of all their passion.

Entrepreneurs are a special breed of people. They have a special something about them that allows them to see things that are not there. Not because they are losing their minds, but because entrepreneurs see things that need to be better, want things to be better, and have the ideas to make that happen. Entrepreneurs are the backbone of society.

Entrepreneurs create. Just think, without entrepreneurs, I would not have written this book. This book would have been a series of stories told from person to person; from generation to generation. There would be no cars, planes, or any other type of transportation. No computers, no printing presses, no fun. As previously stated, entrepreneurs create and consumers buy their creations to make their lives easier.

This book is to promote the entrepreneurial concept and assist people in reaping profits as well as the benefits.

Thank you, entrepreneurs, for enriching my life and for enriching the lives of so many others. Thanks to all of the entrepreneurs of the world. I would like to give special thanks to entrepreneurs like Russell Simmons, Oprah Winfrey, Bill Gates, Sean "P Diddy" Combs, Robert L. Johnson, and Steve Jobs. They have inspired me to go to the next level. Thank you.

Entrepreneurs

What one man can do, another man can do

-Anonymous-

ENTREPRENEURS:

Test to see if you are an entrepreneur

Questions	Yes	No
I have what it takes to own a business		
I have experience in what it is I want to do		
I love serving people		
I influence people well		
I am ready to work longer hours		
I am willing to work harder than I ever have before		
I have a strong support unit		
I know who my competitors are		
I know what my expenses are		
I am willing to take a risk		
I have a passion and the stamina to run a business		
I have a business plan		
I have a well thought out idea		

What is an entrepreneur?

The Dictionary of Business Terms defines an entrepreneur as an "individual who initiates business activity." It also says that "the term is often associated with one who takes business risks." In my opinion, there's so much more to being an entrepreneur. An entrepreneur is a person with an idea, vision, passion, stamina, and strength. Sometimes an entrepreneur is a fortune teller.

The vision is necessary to see what is missing, fill the gaps, and find the niche. Passion provides the fuel to weather the storm and help convince people to believe in your vision. An idea is the spark to solve problems and make things better. I have explained to you what an entrepreneur is in my opinion, but here are some misconceptions about being an entrepreneur and owning your own business.

Misconceptions about being an entrepreneur

1. Some entrepreneurs believe being a business owner means you will have more time. In actuality, you will have less time, especially in the beginning. You will be running around setting up your business, perhaps hiring your team. You may be working an additional job until your business takes off. You may even be doing all of the work by yourself. Sometimes you may not even have time to pick your nose. That's the reality.

2. Being the boss means you know everything. Chances are you don't know everything. You should be very receptive to the ideas and suggestions of other people. Just remember, don't be bossy just because you are the boss. Remember how you felt when you were the employee and you had a bossy supervisor. Dare to be different. Break the cycle.

3. I will have more freedom when I am the boss. Chances are, the higher your position, the less freedom you have. According to John C. Maxwell in the book "360 Degree Leader", and in my own experience, the higher your position, the more responsibility you will have.

4. Now that you have your own business people will respect you. This is one of the biggest misconceptions of them all. In general people respect others for their deeds, and for who they are, not for what they do. John C. Maxwell said it better than I did in the 360 Degree Leader: "People respect disposition not position."

Personally, people who respect me solely for the fact that I have my own business and not for who I am, are not the people I want to be around. I believe they are just looking for how I can benefit them.

What makes an entrepreneur a different type of person?

An entrepreneur is a person that possesses the ability to visualize a need and produces an appropriate solution to accommodate that need. Entrepreneurs are the risk takers of the world, the true movers and shakers. The one thing that separates great successful entrepreneurs from the rest is their ability to conquer their fears. Later, I will briefly discuss some of the reason why entrepreneurs don't succeed (here is a hint: it's the "F" word). In the introduction I listed a group of entrepreneurs and leaders. Here are a few common characteristics that they all share:

• Passionate

Passion keeps you going through the hard times and helps you sell your idea.

• Hard working

A great asset of an entrepreneur is the ability to out work and out think the competition. Hard work will lead you to success. Without work there can be no success. Like Vince Lombardi said, "Success only comes before work in the dictionary."

• Creative

Being creative is an essential part of being an entrepreneur. Creative people are the ones with the ideas. Creative people are the ones that come up with unique solutions to an issue. Creative people think way outside of the box and creative people tend to be thought of as leaders and visionaries.

• Visionary

Visionaries are the ones who figure out the needs of society and create a product or service to satisfy that need. Visionaries are the ones who figure out the direction and course of action that should be taken.

- Resilient

In reality you will have set backs, and tests of your commitment. You may frequently hear "no" to your ideas. If you do not have the ability to come back from a mistake or from hearing the word no, then you may not want to be an entrepreneur. You may want to go and live in the woods by yourself where you will never hear "no". This will be discussed later in the book.

- Great Communicator

Having the ability to communicate is a skill that all aspiring great leaders and entrepreneurs must develop. You will find it very difficult to connect with people, lead, or manage them, or even convey your thoughts effectively to them without the ability to communicate effectively.

- Intelligent

Some will say not all entrepreneurs are intelligent. Don't believe that. There are different ways to measure intelligence. If you were to put together all of the characteristics I have listed above of an entrepreneur, you will probably find a very intelligent person.

Admirable entrepreneurs

In the introduction I listed several people I admire for being on their grind. These people have helped reshape the world as we know it. Their collective contributions have done more for me in terms of inspiration, than any other group of people. Here are a few highlights that will help you understand how they inspired me:

Bill Gates

Bill Gates revolutionized the world as we know it with Microsoft. Gates was able to take an idea and turn it into one of the most powerful companies in the world. He has charities that give to urban and low-income communities, as well as communities throughout the developing world. What Bill Gates did for computers, Russell Simmons did for hip-hop.

Russell Simmons

Hip-hop would not be a part of the world's culture if it were not for Russell Simmons. I don't think he would like that I am saying this, but Simmons is largely responsible for the popularity of hip-hop. Simmons and his team are responsible for Def Jam records, Run DMC, Phat Farm, and Baby Phat. He is also responsible for the hip-hop summit. This a forum of influential people for the hip-hop community that addresses matters of urban communities and hip-hop. Simmons is a mover and a shaker and his integrity is impeccable. He is one of my inspirations as an entrepreneur and as a visionary. He and his team have done more through hip-hop than any other group of people I can think of.

Sean "P Diddy" Combs

Sean "P Diddy" Combs is known for being one of the hardest working men in hip-hop. From back in the day when he was throwing parties at college, to Bad Boy Records, to Sean John clothing, to Sean John cologne, to acting, and so much more. He is a true testament to the saying "being on your grind."

Steven Jobs

Steven Jobs and his team changed the game in computing and the way we listen to and buy music. They successfully brought form and function together and created one of the best computers in the world. Then Apple introduced the iPod which changed the way we listen to music. In junction with the iPod came iTunes which, by now, sells more music than any other store and all stores combined. Wow! I don't know what I would do without my iPod.

Robert L. Johnson

Robert L. Johnson, the former owner of Black Entertainment Television (BET) and the former majority owner of the Charlotte Bobcats. Johnson gave African-Americans a strong media platform in the way of music and television shows. And he was once listed as the richest African-

American in the world. Now Johnson owns RLJ Development (privately owned hotel and real estate investment company) and so many other businesses. Congrats. Keep on grinding.

Oprah Winfrey

I listed Oprah last, but trust me, that is not because I thought of her last; rather it is because she should be in a category all by herself. It is extremely difficult for me to articulate the deep and lasting positive effects of Oprah's endeavors. She serves as a role model to so many and has significantly changed individuals and entire communities... all for the better. Thank you for being you - the woman, the entrepreneur, the icon, and the inspiration.

Ideas/Notes

13
Rules to
Live By

All our dreams can come true, if we have
the courage to pursue them

-Walt Disney-

13 RULES TO LIVE BY:

I was once asked, "If you could guarantee someone success in becoming an entrepreneur, what would you tell them?" I paused for a minute and said, "I will get back to you on that." I really did not have an answer. After looking at several entrepreneurs and leaders, I came up with a list of rules that are applicable across the board. These 13 rules are key factors in becoming successful as an entrepreneur, and also to achieve success in other parts of your life. In short, if you want to be a successful person, follow these rules.

Rule 1. Get off of your ass and take action

Getting off of your ass is one of the critical rules because without action there can be no progress or success. Nothing happens without taking action. I am a strong believer in this rule. Act. I have found if you don't act within the first 24 hours of an idea, chances are you will not do anything. This doesn't mean you have to go out and open your business. You can begin gathering information or create a story board or map out your idea. Getting off your ass is the first step to empowering yourself. Other reasons why you should take action are: You have to put energy into something before you can get energy out of it. So, if you do not put energy into your work it will result in something worse than failure... never making an attempt. Another reason is if you don't act on it right away, someone may beat you to the punch causing you to have future regrets.

Acting now and not procrastinating is one of the many keys to success. In my life I have had good ideas that would have generated a lot of money for me, but because I did not act, I did not reap the benefits from my ideas. For example, years ago, when I was in the fitness industry I came up with some improvements for a piece of fitness equipment. I talked about it but I did not act. I didn't gather information, assess the feasibility of the idea, or take any action to help my idea move from concept to reality. One day, about two or three years later, I walked into the gym and to my surprise

I saw the very same thing I wanted to do. All I wanted to do was kick myself. I have had many experiences with inaction, procrastination, and hesitation. I learned the rule "take action" the hard way. I learned from my own mistakes.

For many years I studied martial arts. So I take a lot of my life's lessons from martial arts. My Sifu (meaning teacher) used to say to me, "Hesitation can kill." He would say this to me because I would be winning while sparring; I would have the person on the ropes, and their hands would drop, yet I wouldn't take the opportunity to deliver the winning blow. I would hesitate. My Sifu said, "One day you will see what I mean when I say "hesitation can kill." He never mentioned that to me again. About four or five months later, I was sparring with someone else and sure enough a similar situation came up. I hesitated. The next thing I realized I was picking myself off the floor. Besides the ringing in my head, I heard my Sifu's voice saying, "Hesitation can kill." Lesson learned.

I apply this to everything I do. I don't wait. If I want to talk to a pretty woman, I do it. If I want to start a business or write a book, I do it. Taking action is very empowering for me. And what is the worst thing that could happen if it doesn't work out? The woman wouldn't be interested me. The business venture wouldn't endure or fail to launch, or the book wouldn't sell. Point being, I stopped hesitating and I am still a winner. Because I took action, I know the result of action. Remember the expression "winners never quit and quitters never win."

I recently read the book "Do You" by Russell Simmons and Chris Morrow. Simmons knew a lot of people with great ideas but they either did not act on their idea or did not stick around long enough to truly capitalize on their ideas. The example above was clearly a case when I did not act. Bad for me, great for someone else.

Here is an example of someone who did not stick around long enough and therefore could not capitalize on the benefit. I was watching the Discovery channel or the History channel. The show had something about Hitler. Some of you will not like the fact that I am using Hitler but it is not to incite ill will or to glorify Hitler. I am just using him as an example. Hitler's engineers came up with the jet fighter and the allied forces fighter planes could not keep up with them. Hitler did not act on the fact that his planes were by far superior to the allied forces planes. That could have been the turning point of the war. This is one case when I can honestly say I am glad someone did not act.

One of the reasons, probably the main reason why people hesitate, is fear. Fear of the unknown, fear of failure, and even fear of success. The book "Who Moved My Cheese" gives a great illustration of fear. The premise of the book is recognizing change and dealing with change. In "Who Moved my Cheese" there were four main characters - two little people and two mice. The little people in the story were intellectually superior at least more superior than the mice. They all lived in a maze and ate the cheese that was left for them. One day the cheese was all gone from the area where they used to go to. Knowing only instinct and using only instinct the mice ventured out to look for more cheese. The little people decided to stay and wait and wait and wait. Guess what caused them to wait? Fear... The fear of not knowing what was out there for them. My suggestion to anyone reading this book is to also read "Who Moved My Cheese."

In business and in life I often use the expression "there is nothing to fear but fear itself." It reminds me that I don't have to fear the unknown. I still have trouble with that concept; so I made a vow to myself and wrote it down on paper and posted it on my wall. Only take action with knowledge, courage, wisdom, information, mental and spiritual clarity, and toughness. With that I will always conquer fear.

There aren't a lot of reasons why people don't act, but there are a whole lot of excuses why they don't act. Here are a few excuses, but before I give them to you, remember the expression about excuses: excuses are like ass-holes; everyone has them and they all stink.

Excuse 1 - The economy. Stop blaming the economy for your lack of action. Don't wait for the economy to turn-around. When you take action, you will help turn the economy around. If nothing else, you will turn your economy around. If you wait for someone else to do it for you then they deserve your money, your accolades, and even your happiness. Just think if there were more businesses opened by entrepreneurs there would be less dependence on major corporations. And, the current economic crisis would not be as bad.

Excuse 2 - I don't have the money. Before you even say that, have you researched government grants? Have you looked into how much you need? Do you even know your credit score? Some of you reading this book will borrow money to get your nails done; for a new pair of sneakers/shoes; on a piece of clothing; but you won't borrow money to fulfill your dream(s). That is crazy to me. My reason is as follows: when you buy a car it depreciates; when you get your nails done they crack or break and you probably could have done them yourself and they would have looked better anyway. We are a nation of spenders; why not spend the money on your dreams. Remember if you can put it on your ass, it is not an asset.

Excuse 3 - Time. I don't have the time. So make the time. Invest one or two hours a day in your business and watch it take a life of its own. There are so many entrepreneurs out there that are single parents and they go to school and work another job. So time should not be an issue for most of us.

There are many more excuses why people don't act but those are the top three I have heard. After saying this, I will say that opportunity is like lightning in that it never strikes in the same place twice, but you can be assured it will strike again. The reason is that sometimes it's just not the right time for you to seize the opportunity, or you missed it. Rest and be assured, if you are persistent, work hard, stay positive, the opportunity will present itself again. You just have to recognize it and not hesitate the next time. Some people will dare to tell you that opportunity doesn't appear every day. I suggest you tell those people to go to hell. Don't keep company with negative people. Their negativity may be contagious. Keep in mind what I tell myself: The opportunity to work, learn, love, grow, and even make money happens every day. It's just our ability to recognize opportunity that's the issue.

Rule 2. Don't share information right away

A lot of people would tell you to tell others about your business idea. I am a little different. If you have a great idea or one you believe is great, initially keep it to yourself. You will look and walk as though you have something good to say and that will attract people to you. And because people are naturally curious, it makes them want to speak to you to find out what you have to say. In addition to that, it gives you the time to figure out whether your new idea is something you really want to pursue.

When it's time to divulge your great idea, be careful who you tell it to. As much as people will tell you how great your ideas are, some of them will secretly send negative vibes your way and that may be enough to cancel out the positive energy you have. Remember some people never want you to be higher than they are.

Only tell your most trusted people or person; the most positive person. Also, make sure their trust has the ability to ground you; make sure they will support your efforts. And of equal importance, make sure they can keep your idea quiet until you are ready to release the information. Then look out world, here you come! When the time comes and you have built up enough positive energy that no matter what anyone says or does can stop you, then, you should tell other people.

Rule 3. You can't do everything yourself

A mistake some entrepreneurs make is thinking they can do everything themselves. That is a recipe for a certain disaster. Remember you have a brilliant idea but without the correct people around you, it will be tough for you to realize your idea. In the book "17 Indisputable Laws of Leadership", John C. Maxwell talks about the rule of the mountain, which in essence, states the larger the goal, the more people you need.

For example, you have a great concept to open a company that caters to the elderly. You developed the products and services yourself but you may not know how to implement your ideas or bring your products and services to the market. The people you have around you have to know how to bring your product to the market.

Another scenario - you have just come up with the ultimate widget. You know there is a market for your product. But you have no idea about business formation, no idea of administration, and you don't have management skills. Launching a business without having acquired those skill sets will spell disaster, but having people around you that can fill the gaps will at least give you a fighting chance. Not doing things by yourself will give you a different perspective. There are other times when you may need someone else in your corner and they can be a great assistance to you and your business.

For a lot of us we don't like the idea of having an attorney. Some attorneys have created a bad name for their industry - making money off of peoples' misfortune. Which reminds me of a joke once told to me a couple of winters ago. "It is so cold outside that all of the attorneys have their hands in their own pockets." That joke may be corny but it is the perception of a lot of people. However, attorneys can be a great asset for you and your business endeavors.

An attorney's legal advice is necessary to counter mishaps. There will be people who may try to take your idea or you may find yourself in some type of lawsuit. Face it, shit happens and having quality legal advice is like using a condom - "added protection."

Accountants are another great asset to have similar to an attorney - they can provide you with great business advice such as business formation. An accountant may be better at deciding which business entity best suits your financial needs and goals.

Face it, there are a lot of things that can be said about accountants and attorneys, good and bad. If you have experienced bad, get over them, and move on; make another connection.

All of that said, as an entrepreneur, you may not have the funds readily available to have a law firm on retainer or even to hire an accountant. But there are a lot of law firms out there who, were you to pay X amount of dollars per year, would provide you with legal counsel (this is at a minimal cost). Accounting firms may have similar services or you may find the discount tax service centers to assist you (If not, that is a great idea for a business).

Another way to get help is use your support group, which will be discussed in the next rule. Someone in your support group may be a lawyer, accountant, or a banker. Offer to take them out for a bite to eat in exchange for some information or pay them something even if you don't have a lot or you can't give them the normal fee. I strongly believe in paying for services rendered. That way no one can say you used them, plus you will feel better.

Rule 4.   Support units

A support group is great for many different reasons. They provide a platform of support and counsel. They also let you know you are not alone. In your entrepreneurial pursuit you may feel alone. There will be many trials in your quest to get your business afloat. Some of the trials will test your very essence; some will make you wonder if you can continue; some of them will even test your ability to function. Remember, trials are not there to set you up for failure. Trials are put there to test your desire. Some will say trials are us catching up to our past negative thoughts. Whatever the case may be, they can help you appreciate obtaining your goal. There are many different examples of how having a support group will help. When I was younger, I used to hear: "God will never place anything on your shoulders that what you cannot handle." Believe it.

[E.g. 1] Quitting smoking may be one of the hardest things a person can do. There are places one can go to and groups one can join to quit smoking. These group members understand being in a group can help you quit. As previously stated, support groups provide a platform of support and counsel which makes it easier for a person to honor their commitment and quit smoking

[E.g. 2] When studying [for a big test], it is often better doing it in groups. There may be people in the group that can share a different perspective if an issue or a conflict in opinion should arise.

[E.g. 3] In my personal experience with support groups, I have gone out on many business ventures; some worked out and some did not. Without the support of family and friends it would have been even more difficult than it was. To be honest with you, I would not have been able to write this book if my family and friends would not have been there for me.

I would lock myself in a room for several hours per day without talking or seeing anyone, sometimes not even eating. My family would make sure I ate, took a break, and my friends would make me go out. That's what having a good support unit will do. Remember, no one gets anywhere by themselves. You may bear witness to the accomplishments of the individual, but there is always some type of support group behind them. I cannot stress enough just how important it is to have a support group. The following are some examples of what having a support group can do.

When used properly, support/networking groups may prove to be more beneficial than your friends or family.

Think about what really goes on to elect a president besides a catchy catch-phrase and tons of money. Think about how many people are involved in that process. It starts off very much like an entrepreneur would start a business.

First, you have a person with a vision on how to make things better for the country. Then that person has to put together a team of people that believe in his/her vision. Next, they have to form a strategy. Next, they need to acquire the funding to start the campaign (business venture). Then they have to sell it to the public and the rest is history. This was an abbreviated version but I am certain you get the point.

Another example of a support group is a networking group. Networking groups are especially important for entrepreneurs. There are rules for networking groups:

1. You have to add value.
2. You have to have something to offer.
3. Build your network before you need them.
4. Maintain it by being personal and stay in touch with them via lunch dates/meetings, e-mail, and an occasional phone call.

Some of you reading this book may say, "I don't have a support unit. I have to do everything myself. I am my own cheerleader." I hear you and understand, but there are ways to combat this issue. There are plenty of networking groups out there, virtual and otherwise. Join a few. Get a feel for which one you like, and then share when you feel it's appropriate.

Just to re-emphasize family: Your family and friends as a source of networking. I am sure they know someone or know of someone that may be able to point you in the right direction. Remember six degrees of separation is real and in your case it may even be less than that.

Rule 5. One thing at a time

There are plenty of people who come up with good ideas. And they try to work on all of their ideas at the same time. That is a very difficult task to embark on. If one works on several ideas at once how can you effectively put 100 percent of your energy and your concentration into all of them? I have been faced with having multiple ideas and I have come up with some techniques that worked for me.

My suggestion is that you write all of your ideas down and think about them. The idea you are most passionate about is the one you should go with. Saying that is not to say that you should totally disregard the other ideas. Remember you wrote them down. Once you have finished the one you are most passionate about, then you can start the next one.

Another idea is to write down the pros and cons of all of your ideas. The one that has the most pros is the one you go with.

Think about a time when you were at work and you were working on several projects at the same time. Then your boss came up to you and asked you to begin working on another project. To top it off, one of your co-workers' was out sick and you had to finish up his or her work. How effective were you doing all of that? Now multiply that by ten. That's how it will feel like when you have your own business.

Rule 6. Prioritize

A great idea can be implemented at any time and will always work in any economic climate. A good idea will work if the timing is right. An ok idea even needs better timing because it will be harder to convince people to believe in it, but it can still work. I use the following strategies when I have a difficult time prioritizing.

I create a list of ideas, concepts, etc; once I have the list created, I identify the one thing I would do for free. That's the one I choose to go with first. In terms of duties and obligations, create two lists. The first list is all of the things that require your direct attention. The second, the ones you can delegate to someone else, perhaps a person in your support group.

When I was writing this book I had a lot of things I was working on including a lecture series, a leadership book, as well as working on developing various workshops for the youth in my local area.

I wrote a list of ideas. Once I had the list of ideas, it was time to prioritize which one I was going to put into action first. Here is my thought process: I would do all of them for free so that concept was not going to help me. All of them, in my opinion, were good ideas and the timing was correct. So what I had to do was think of a way all of them could work together. I wrote the entrepreneur book, created the lecture series, and then the book on leadership. Last but not least I developed the seminar for the youth in my local area. One concept validated the other. This worked for me and can work for you but the most important thing I did was to take action. I made the list.

Prioritizing will help your project management, leadership skills, and life skills which are key components of starting and maintaining a successful business venture or having a successful life. Setting dates for a task to be accomplished is important whenever portion of the project should be completed. This will give you a sense of accomplishment and empowerment. Even if the project doesn't get completed you can learn and make adjustments for the next project. Remember, every accomplishment takes you one step closer to making your dream come true. And every mishap makes you appreciate your accomplishments more.

Rule 7. Dealing with setbacks

Look at setbacks as a check. Setbacks are reality checks to see if you have the balls to continue. The more checks you have in your pocket the more confidence you will have in yourself.

Learn to deal with setbacks. Put your setbacks on paper and use them as a learning experience. Or you can do what I do - create a journal of setbacks. This will be your own way of creating a log of learning; a self tutorial for success. Setbacks are not all bad, although they may seem to be for an entrepreneur. Keep in mind, in all businesses, all people have setbacks. It's not that you have setbacks, [but] it's how you get over them. If you use your setbacks as a learning experience and you do not quit, you have already won. Let your support unit help you get through the setbacks. And don't allow your setbacks to take you away from who you are.

Rule 8. Never compromise your integrity

Your integrity defines who you are, and who you are will dictate what you do. Never compromise your integrity. You will have trials that test who you are and what you want for your company. Always remember it's your dream and you can make it a reality.

Some people may have questionable integrity. At least that is how we may perceive it. For example if you are the type of person whose sole purpose and intent is to make money at all costs, you may lie, cheat, and steal, and will not have compromised your integrity. By no means am I advocating doing those things to get money but it is an example of integrity. You may end up with money but not true wealth - that is the trust, loyalty, and love of others. I firmly believe in karma; what goes around comes around. So I believe in giving my best to ensure I receive the best the world has to offer.

Every great leader, whether in business or politics, has a certain amount of uncompromising integrity. In my opinion uncompromising integrity is the very trait that separates good leaders from great leaders. My personal favorite is Russell Simmons who is one of the largest icons in urban culture. In his book "Do You", Simmons was offered a lot of money to comprise the integrity of his vision for Phat Farm (his clothing line). Simmons was asked to change his line by adding clothing that did not fit his vision in exchange for a shit load of money. He did not compromise his vision, and his clothing line prospered. That does not always happen - things turning out well financially. However, if at the end of the day you don't have a financial windfall but you haven't compromised your beliefs - you can hold your head high. You still have your integrity. If you have not read Simmons' book, read it. It is very insightful.

I have experienced the opportunity to compromise my integrity. I have a business consulting company where I consult in areas ranging from business plans and marketing strategies to leadership coaching. There is one thing I say, every project I work on is customized. One day a personal friend asked me for help with a marketing strategy for his non-profit. The type of non-profit was the same as the one I just finished working on. It would have been very easy for me to use the old marketing strategy and just change a few facts and figures. No one would have known if I used the old strategy, but I would never compromise my integrity. Instead, I started from scratch and created a new marketing strategy. My friend was pleased with the outcome and my integrity was uncompromised.

In the same vein, expand your sense of integrity to your company. Create a mission statement and set of guiding principles that serve as the framework for all actions and business decisions in your company. Think of this as an unwavering statement and set of principles that sum up what your company stands for and how it does business. Mean it. Say it. Live it. That's integrity.

Rule 9. Take responsibility

Responsibility is a trait great leaders and great Generals have. I want to challenge you to think of business as war. You are the General and your employees are the soldiers. Wars are won by the soldiers but lost by the Generals. The General comes up with the strategy; the soldiers execute the orders. So the battle is won or lost by the decisions the General gives. The prosperity of your business will rise and fall on what you do and the decisions you make. Be responsible and take responsibility.

Recently I went into a store where my friend was the manager. As soon as I had entered the store, I was greeted with a bad attitude. I almost turned around and walked out. The greeter acted as though she was doing me a favor by asking, "May I help you?" I decided not to leave and asked for the manager instead. While I was waiting for him, I began to look around the store and noticed all of the employees were in a pissy mood. I put on my leadership hat. Then I saw my friend. He was running around like a chicken with its head cut off. He went to one employee and took her work away and did it himself. Then he did the same thing to another employee. After about 20 minutes he finally gets to me and said, "What's up Rob? You can see its crazy around here."

I said, "Listen here, if you keep this up, you will burn yourself out and you will find yourself, by yourself. Your employees will quit, just before you lose your customers. Then you will get fired." By the puzzled look on his face, I could tell he did not understand. I told him to stop for a minute and look around. I pointed out that his entire team was in a pissy mood. They are going to drive away customers. I know because I almost left.

I said, "Listen I am going to give you some unsolicited advice." He nodded. I pointed out that he was running around like a chicken with its head cut off. This makes it look as though you are out of control. His employees were in a pissy mood; perhaps it was because they were bored or maybe for another reason. Maybe you should stop doing everything and stop micro-managing them. Let them do what they were hired to do. Stop having your hands in everything and micro-managing everyone. It gives the appearance you don't trust your employees to do their jobs, and on top of that you disempowered them. Next I asked, "Are you always like that?" You already know his reply.

My friend said thank you, but these people have no clue and they are incompetent. I ask them to do things as small as call the cable company to see why the cable is not on for my customers and they can't even do that. After that he gave more examples. They half-ass fold the clothes; they come in late; and take extra long breaks. They barely tend to my customers and when they do, they have an attitude. There is more, but I am sure you get the point. This guy blames the team for his lack of leadership.

First I said, "Wow! Do you really think your people are incompetent?" The response was "Yes." Then I explained, "You have to decide whether you are a manager or a leader." He asked, "What do you mean?" I explained that managers get the process done through people. Leaders inspire people to go above and beyond the call of duty and that wasn't happening. If you are not inspiring your people to go above and beyond or you're not able to manage people to get a task done, plus your sales are going down, you may need to assess the way you communicate with your people. Sometimes trying to get people to realize what they are doing wrong without hitting them over the head with a brick is very hard.

In order to lead people effectively you first have to care about people. Once your employees see you genuinely care, they in turn will care. Then learn a new way to communicate your needs and desires. Empower them, don't micro-manage them. And you have to accept responsibility for your own actions. He asked, "What actions?" and said, "I tell them to sell more, so they should sell more. And if they don't want to work, they should go home. They can be replaced." I asked him, "Are you a fan of any professional sports?" He said, "Yes, baseball and basketball." I said, "Here you go, if the whole team is not happy and not producing in sports, what happens?" He said, "They get new players." I said, "No they get a new manager. Get it? Take your head out of your ass and take responsibility for the role you have played in your employees' behavior."

Rule 10. Be grateful

Every morning when you wake up, list the things you are grateful for and every night before you go to sleep, say what you are grateful for. Both lets the higher power know you acknowledge the gifts you are given. There are so many reasons why a person should be grateful but especially an entrepreneur. Be grateful for the talent you have to develop great ideas; your passion for creating; for your ability to lead; and for the support you receive. Be grateful for your setbacks; they serve as learning experiences. I don't mean to sound sappy, but we all have things to be grateful for, and not doing so rips a hole in the very fabric of our humanity. A lack of gratitude taints the soul.

Here is a brief list of the things I have to be grateful for:

1. My health
2. Family, friends and my support groups
3. You reading this book
4. My business
5. My passion

Rule 11. Stress relief

A lot of stress is associated with being an entrepreneur and starting your own business - long hours, difficult projects, and employee issues, along with the stresses of everyday life. One way I cope with stress is to change my perception. If something does not work out, I don't look at that as a failure; I look at it as a learning experience. When stress starts to get to me, I go to the gym, or if working out is not for you, try taking Russell Simmons' advice and take a yoga class or meditate. I agree with the meditating part. I do it for a couple of minutes periodically throughout the day to recharge. I also go for walks to clear my head or I sit in a quiet room. There are often times when I listen to music. Basically in short, you should find something that works to relax you. Your mental and physical health is more important than the health of your business.

Some people would say don't take your work home nor should you work from home. Their rationale is your home is your sanctuary and the energy of work has no place in the home. I say it is very difficult for some entrepreneurs not to work from home. In fact, it is very likely a lot of their businesses will be conducted at home, but you have to find a balance.

Here is my take on working at home. First, the energy of work is good and positive because no long term success can come without work. Second, if you have children they need to develop good working habits. What better way to teach them than by setting an example?

I will leave you with this: The way you perceive things can reduce your stress. If you change your perception, you change your mind and you grow and flourish.

Rule 12. Give back

Let's face it, you are not going to get where you need to be, by yourself. It just does not happen that way, unless you hit the lottery. What are the chances of that really happening? Which means someone helped you. You have to help others and by helping others, you will continue to receive blessings. Remember karma - what goes around comes around.

Rule 13. Positive attitude

A positive attitude may be one of the most valuable assets an entrepreneur possesses. A positive attitude can and will take you far. Positive attitudes have helped people overcome insurmountable odds. A positive attitude will help you connect with people. It will help your vision, your spirit, and your mental wellness. Positive attitudes have helped people walk again, run again, and win.

Ideas/Notes

Ideas/Notes

Dealing With Fear

Nothing to fear but fear itself
-Franklin Delano Roosevelt-

DEALING WITH FEAR:

You are your worst enemy. Once you learn to get out of your own way, you will truly have no limits to what you can accomplish. Fear is one of those things we all have. Fear, if used properly, can keep you sharp and keep you safe. Fear unchecked can be paralyzing.

3

My mother has helped me deal with fear. I told my mother I was thinking of moving out of the state but I was nervous. So she did something that made me feel a little silly. She reduced it to the ridiculous. The conversation went a little like this:

Me:	Mom I want to move but I am very nervous.
My mother:	Why?
Me:	I have responsibilities here.
My mother:	So take care of them, and then go.
Me:	My favorite aunt is getting old and she needs me.
My mother:	No matter where you go you will be less than 24 hrs away.
Me:	I don't have the money.
My mother:	Plan and save. Is there anything else? Are you still nervous?
Me:	No

I said no but I realized it wasn't nerves; I was just scared of the unknown. You know mothers always know their children and mine was no different. A couple of days later my mother called, and said, what is the worst thing that can happen? It doesn't work out. If it doesn't you can always come back - it's just that simple. And at least you would have tried. I took her advice and it worked out. Crazy, right?

Reducing things to the ridiculous often helps me when I have a difficult decision to make. And, it helps me get to the root of an issue.

Ways of dealing with fear

There are many other ways to deal with fear and there are many ways I deal with my own fears. The first thing I do is to identify what it is and where it comes from. Then I write down the worst thing that can happen. Once I have reduced it to the root, it makes it easier to deal with, and often my fears disappear. You see, I have already dealt with the worst possibility and can act on solutions. Someone once told me it's not that you have an issue, nor is it about how many issues you have. It's about how you deal with them. And that's the difference between success and failure. Keep it moving. The last thing, and this may sound corny, have faith. Have faith in yourself. Most of all have faith in God or whatever you call your higher power.

I have tried many methods of dealing with fear. Here is one way that may assist you:

- First realize that fear is good but can be controlled.
- Then take a piece of paper and jot down what you are fearful of.
- Then write out the worst possible outcome.
- Then write what would happen if you don't face your fear.

What youth affords you

When I was in my twenties, I was bold, fierce like a lion. Whatever I wanted I went out and got it. At some point I lost it. I am not sure where or when, but I lost my bold sense of daring. In my thirties, I was reflecting on my life and I asked myself, "What happened to me, where did I go?" I had an "oh shit" moment. I had some business ventures that did not turn out the way I wanted. I had not achieved the success I so often dreamed about. And, there I was afraid of failing. I realized it would be impossible for me to be in my twenties again but I knew I had to regain that boldness.

I reopened my consulting company. I had no money and no time, but so what? I did it. I consulted for free. I gave motivational talks to anyone who would listen. I wrote business plans and marketing strategies for free, not because I did not need or want the money, but because that's what I enjoy doing. Guess what? It all worked out for the best. And, I have to say I am a lot happier now than I ever was in the past. The way I dealt with my fear of failing was to adopt the Nike motto "Just Do it."

If you have fears about starting your own business get over them and start it - "Just do it." Everyone has fears. The difference between successful people and others is that successful people face their fears.

Ideas/Notes

Ideas/Notes

Starting Your Business

Get off of your ass and make it happen
-Robert D. Pettiford-

STARTING YOUR BUSINESS:

I have an idea for a business, what do I do?

1. Ask yourself: Am I serious?
2. Ask yourself: Do I have a passion for this or am I just talking?
3. Figure out if your business idea is legal.
4. Find facts: Get all of the information concerning your business (i.e. competition, substitutes).
5. Incorporate your business, get any patents, or if necessary, copyrights, whichever is right for your idea.
6. Develop a business plan.
7. Find investors if needed. Launch your business, maintain it, and grow your business.

Starting your business

Deciding the type of legal entity is extremely important and its level of importance is second only to getting off of your ass and getting starting. There are really only three types of businesses (1) Sole proprietorship (2) Partnership (3) Corporations. There are sub-divisions in partnerships and corporations that will be discussed. Before I get into the business plan types here are a few factors you should consider and hold in the forefront of your mind when making the decision to start a business:

- Personal liability
- Cost of maintenance and time
- Intellectual property
- Size and complexity
- Taxes
- Any regulatory requirements that are imposed from the local state and federal government
- Barriers to entry if any

This section is not meant to replace professional help. Check with your attorney and accountant before making the final decision.

Sole proprietorship:

This is a business that only has a single owner. The following is a list of characteristics a sole proprietor has:

- One (sole) owner
- The owner has total liability
- May have lower taxes
- Relatively easy to form
- Less government regulation
- All business income treated as personal income
- If the owner dies the business dies

Starting a Sole Proprietorship

First, check to see if you need to register with your local municipality. I believe it is always better to register a business whether you have to or not. Registering a business provides your potential customers with a little more security. They will know you have a legitimate business.

Partnership:

A partnership is a business that has more than one owner. And there are two types of partnerships, general and limited.

General Partnership
- Hard to add or delete a partner
- Owners have total liability
- Easier to form than a corporation but harder to form than a sole proprietorship
- May have lower taxes
- If an owner dies the business dies

Limited partnership

A limited partnership is pretty much the same as a general partnership with the following exceptions:

1. Partners have a say based on the amount of their investment and will receive profits based on the amount they invest.
2. Upon death of a partner the business can still survive.
3. Some states do not recognize LLP's and the states that do may limit it to doctors, lawyers, and accountants.
4. Each partner is not liable for the actions of the other partner (in a lot of cases)

Starting a partnership

*   You must register your partnership
*   File a Doing Business As (DBA) or an assumed name if needed

Corporation:

Corporations are legal entities. Corporations can exist even after the owner dies. As a legal entity, corporations have the right to own other businesses and properties, incur debt such as loans, credit cards, etc. Although, banks tend to make the principals of the business be a personal guarantor for any type of loan (especially for newly formed corporations). In essence, there is only one type of corporation, and any sub-divisions of a corporation is really about taxation. A corporation may have a non-profit status or a sub-chapter S. If you are thinking about opening a corporation you may want to consider which one best suits your needs. And again, contact your Attorney or Accountant for advice.

Corporation (C-Corp)

*   Limited stockholder financial responsibility
*   Takes more time to form and is more expensive to start than other legal entities and may be more expensive to run. There tends to be more paperwork than other types of businesses.

- Double taxed. The corporation pays taxes on profits, and any profits taken out in terms of dividends are taxed as well.
- May receive tax breaks in certain states

S-Corporation or subchapter S

- There is a tax on the firm's profit rather than on the dividend.
- Stockholders pay corporate federal tax at their personal rate.
- Some states may not recognize S-Corporation
- Starting an S-Corporation
- Must file articles of incorporation
- Must obtain EIN (Employer Identification Number)
- Have by-laws
- Board of directors
- Regularly scheduled monthly meetings

Non-Profit

The most complicated of all corporations to start is a non-profit, because of the amount of paperwork involved and how detailed the wording has to be. There are some similarities to a C-Corp., for example:

- Must file articles of incorporation
- Must obtain EIN (Employer Identification Number)
- Have by laws
- Have a board of directors
- Regularly scheduled monthly meetings

Here is how a non-profit differs from a C-Corp.:

- Filing for non-profit status
- Length of time to file
- Taxed differently

There are different types of non-profit statuses one may obtain, but remember they are listed in a manner that allows for certain taxation purposes and what they are allowed to do. The one I believe most people are familiar with is the 501(c)3 which includes educational and other charitable institutions. The 501(c)3 status has about 26 subdivisions. To familiarize yourself with non-profit organization statuses you may want to consult with an attorney.

You have your idea, now the next step is to secure your business name. Go online and research your chosen business name. If you have not chosen a name for your business, then try to pick one that is close to your heart; for example, my consulting business is named after me, "R D Pettiford Consulting". Some might say that is egocentric. I named the business after me because it gives me more of a personal stake. If I put my name on it then I have to make it the best I possibly can. My family's name is on it and I would not want to smear my family's name.

Now that you have decided on a legal entity that fits your needs, you have to figure out the state of incorporation. You may want to seek the advice of a lawyer at this point. It may cost you more than money if you make a mistake here. It may cost you valuable time.

In the meantime, get a piece of paper and write down what you are going to do. Write the pros and cons of what you want to do as well as the pros and cons of each type of legal entity and pick the one that best suits your needs.

This part can be very tricky - some states offer tax incentives for having your business. My suggestion to you is to visit those states' web sites and review the requirements. Here are some of the reasons why certain states may be advantageous (I would like to say there is nothing like having the advice of a qualified accountant or lawyer).

The advantages of incorporating in Delaware

Delaware attracts many companies because incorporating is a fairly simple process.

- The shareholder's stock is not taxed in the same manner as other states.
- Personal information about the principal is not required, i.e. names and addresses.
- The cost is extremely low.

The advantages of incorporating in Nevada

- One person can hold all offices.
- Formation process is easy.
- No state corporate tax on profits

There are more advantages, but to gain true insight on state incorporation requirements, seek professional help. And again, if you can't afford an attorney or an accountant or you don't have one in your support group, there are plenty of good books out there on the subject.

Websites

People always ask me, "Do I need a website?" My answer to them is "yes". Websites are electronic business cards. A website adds convenience for your company. They allow, you to reach a broader client base and, for some, they make your business more credible. A website allows potential customers to find out more about you and your company in the privacy of their own homes. Think about all of the reasons why you go to check out companies online. I am sure you will understand the value a website can add.

Intellectual property

Intellectual property is a broad term used to cover the legal right of property created by the mind, which includes music, inventions, words, art logos or symbols. You may be familiar with copyright, patents, trademarks, industrial design rights or trade secrets. This book will not go into too much detail about intellectual property. For more details on the subject you may want to enlist the assistance of legal counsel or purchase books on the subject. You can also contact the United States Patent and Trademark office by visiting their website www.uspto.gov.

This section is designed to make you more familiar with the terms. The following is a brief description of what each of the previously mentioned terms are:

Copyright

It is a legal protection which covers such things as books, movies, software, pictures, etc. For example, the people creating the bootleg CD's and DVD's are breaking the copyright laws. They do not have permission to reproduce it from the artists or the company that puts it out. Copyright laws protect the work for the life of the author, plus 70 years.

For more information on copyright laws you can go to the United States Copyright Office's web site: www.copyright.gov.

Patents

A patent is the right to own an invention for a given time by the government. The time span of a patent can last anywhere from 14 years to 20 years depending if it is utility or plant or design. My suggestion, if you are going to need your intellectual property patented, is that you first visit the United States Patent and Trademark Office's web-site: www.uspto.gov.

Trademark

Trademarks cover phrases, symbols, designs, or any other object that distinguishes a company. For example, Puma sneaker uses the puma. The time span of a trademark can be forever as long as the owner doesn't stop using it. For more information on trademarks, go to the United States Patent and Trademark Offices at www.uspto.gov.

Getting the money

Now you have your business plan, you may need to secure financing. There are a lot of ways to obtain funding. Friends, family, personal investments i.e. your 401k, investments, stocks, bonds, etc. But let's keep it real; after the market crashed, a lot of people just don't have the funds in their personal investments. If you are not as fortunate to have invested your money, then you cannot look there either. Some entrepreneurs just are not savers; they are spenders, risk takers. That is not to say entrepreneurs don't save at all. It's to say some may have lost their money in a business venture that did not go the way they planned.

There are also other avenues you can use - banks, grants, micro lenders, venture capitalists, and angel hair investments. This next section of the book will explain first what they are and then the pros and cons of using inside sources and outside sources to fund your business.

Banks

Banks have a certain criteria to lend money. You need to check that out before investing too much time looking into obtaining a business loan from a bank. Remember these few facts about banks and who they loan money to.

We have just experienced one of the worse recessions in history. Companies had been laying off people left and right. Banks and their lending practices were seriously scrutinized by the government and hurt because of the economy. All of that said, banks are more careful to whom they lend money to and why. The end result is that it makes it harder for regular folks to get business loans.

With all of that said banks still practice the same old lending policies - lending funds to businesses that don't really need it. It's funny I would say that, but its true and here is why. Some banks have the policy that a business has to be in existence anywhere from 3 to 5 years and show a positive cash flow to qualify for a loan. Stop right here and think for a second - you have a business; you have positive cash flow; your company has been in existence for 3 to 5 years. Why do you need a business loan? Some may say that they want to expand; some may need to do repairs; some may just want to go on vacation at the company's expense. Whatever the reason may be, if you saved and prepared for the future, there may not be a need to take out a loan. Just something to consider.

Anyway, if you have good credit and a home, substantial savings, and/or some other instrument of value, you may qualify for a loan. I have seen a great deal of good business ideas fail at this point because a bank failed to extend a loan. Some people think just because they have their accounts at a particular bank, that bank has to give them a loan. So not true.

If everything looks good on paper and you meet most of the bank's criteria but you have not been in existence for the required amount of time, some banks will ask if you have a business plan. If you do, they will give your business plan to the Small Business Administration (SBA). And at the end of the day that is something you could have done yourself. In no way am I saying you should not deal with a bank to get your business loan. I am only stating what I have experienced. Actually, if you have a banker in your support group, in particular, someone that does business development or is in lending, they may have intimate knowledge of how a business plan should read and the process of obtaining a loan through their institution.

Grants

First, what are grants? Grants are funds that are set aside by the government or corporations to assist individuals or companies in obtaining something. The person or the company usually doesn't have to pay back the grant. To help ensure success in the grant process, it is always helpful to obtain a grant writer. Grants can be tricky. If you miss one word or leave out something, you may not get the grant. Some organizations seem to have people whose sole purpose is to disqualify you from getting a grant. They look for content, spelling, anything you can imagine, and some things you can't. If you are going to write your own grant, you may consider buying a book and/or taking classes for grant writing. I am not saying you can't get a grant without doing any of the previous, but I am a big advocate of leaving it to the professionals. If you are an entrepreneur that has a talent for writing, I would say go ahead and write the grant application. It's worth a try. You can always contact or visit the organizations' website to make sure you are on the right track. Actually, some would even suggest you do that. After all, they know what they want and how they want it. So if you are going to write your own, make it happen. Be like Nike, "Just do it".

The following are some sites you can check to search for grants and grant writers:

www.grants.gov
www.fdncenter.org

There are a lot more sites you can go to, to get grant information. You can also get books on grants.

Ideas/Notes

Your Business Plan

Good fortune is what happens when opportunity
meets with planning

-Thomas Alva Edison-

YOUR BUSINESS PLAN:

Now that you have chosen the state you are going to incorporate in, it's time to figure out how you are going to obtain funding. There are several ways to obtain funding but in order to do so you must have a business plan. This section will discuss the importance of a business plan; who it should be given to and why. It will also provide a very simple outline of a business plan and explain the individual parts.

The importance of a business plan

A business plan is the foundation that describes the type of business, money required, target market, etc. In short, it's an articulated and well communicated version of your dream.

Common Misconceptions

"I really don't need a business plan, I know what I want"

I would like to dispel the notion that a business plan is not needed. Business plans are a great tool for you as an entrepreneur. Even if you don't need financing, you still need a business plan. It helps maintain your focus. It puts your vision into words. It shows that you have thought out your idea. A business plan will also show how well you can manage a business. It really does a lot.

A specific length is required

There is no specific length for a business plan. Some people make business plans that are way too long. I have seen business plans that were 75 or even 100 pages long. Business plans come in many lengths, shapes, and forms. I have always believed a business plan should be long enough to cover all possible aspects of the business in a well communicated way. Simultaneously, it should be short enough to keep the reader's attention.

"All business plans are the same"

All business plans are not the same and may or may not have the same topics or the same content. No two businesses are the same. If you are writing a business plan with the hopes of raising funds, you should first do your research. Find out what the investor is looking for and then tailor your business plan for that investor.

Parts of a business plan

I would like to start this section by stating you may not need every item mentioned. Remember, the business plan conveys your thoughts in a concise, well communicated manner that keeps the readers' attention.

This section is designed to assist you in understanding the components of a business plan. There are a lot of great books around to help you write a business plan or you can hire someone to write one for you. You can even buy software to assist you in writing your business plan. But in my opinion, there is nothing like a customized business plan written by a professional. I may be biased because my company develops business plans; however, having seen business plans written by an unseasoned person, I can say it needed a lot of work.

Title page

Tells the reader your company name and who wrote the business plan. I like to make the cover as exciting as possible without overwhelming the reader.

Table of contents

Just like in a book the table of contents tells readers what to expect, and is often looked at with intense scrutiny. The reader looks at the table of contents to make sure everything they want to read will be covered.

Executive summary:

The executive summary is a brief snapshot of all of the parts of your business plan. It's how you are going to sell your idea; who you are going to sell it to; how much capital is required (if any); the payback period; and so much more. The interesting thing about executive summaries is that it appears first but is often written last. This ensures it properly summarizes your business plan.

If you do not have a good executive summary, chances are your business plan will not be read. And you will have to go back to the drawing board. If that happened to you and you quit, guess what? You failed. If you did not quit and saw this as an opportunity for you to learn and grow, you are ahead of the game. Also remember opportunities are like lightning; it may not strike in the same place twice, but it will strike again. The only question remaining is: Are you going to be ready when opportunity presents itself again?

What should be included in an executive summary?

- Company profile
- The product or service you are offering
- The management team and profile of the management team
- Any financing requirements
- Projection i.e. sales, profits, net income
- Use of the funds
- Precise and concise business description
- The competitive advantage (why now, why this business)

Business description

This section is a detailed outline of the company and the products and services offered. This section includes the following:

- Mission statement
- Conception/history of the business
- Legal form of the company
- Products and services offered by your company
- Competitive advantage

Market analysis

The market analysis is the portion of the business plan that allows the entrepreneur to show the reader that he or she understands the market and the opportunities that exist within that market.

- A complete overview of the proposed industry
- Your target markets (demographics)
- Competition
- Barriers to entry

Leadership/Management team

Often the management team is what will keep your company afloat during hard times and make it a thriving company when times are good. This section explains your reasons for having the management team you have and their credentials. This section also shows the reader that you and your team can and will effectively lead/manage the business. Sometimes when you start a business you may not have the resources to have a management team. In that case, you have to show your ability to lead/manage the firm yourself. But remember to use your support group. Make sure you include these sections when describing your leadership/management team.

- Background, credentials, and duties of each person involved
- Structure of the organization
- Ownership
- Board of directors if need be

Competitive Analysis

This section lists and evaluates your competitors. It lists their products and services as well as their strengths and weaknesses.

- The competition: who are they? What do they do and how? Percent of the market they have.
- Fluctuations in the industry

Products and Services

This section explains the products and services you're going to offer and how you are going to get them into the market.

- A detailed description of your products or services
- Product placement
- Future products and services, if any

Marketing and Sales

This section states how you are going to get your product or service to your market.

- Marketing strategy
- Sales strategy
- Marketing mix
- Sales forecast

Operations

This section is a brief overview of the tactics for implementing the business plan. This section shows the reader, you understand how to implement the business plan.

- Key personnel
- Organizational structure
- The structure of your customer service
- Facilities required

Financials

To the investor this is the "make sense" portion of the business plan. It shows, in no uncertain terms, that the entrepreneur understands the money.

- Comments and assumptions
- Start-up costs
- Starting balance sheet
- Profit and loss projection
- Balance sheet projection (3 to 5 years)

Evaluation

I like to add this section. It shows the reader how the start-up will be monitored.

- Monitoring and evaluation strategy

Appendices

This section shows the reader the references used. If the reader is looking for more details, it can found in this is the section.

- Articles
- Statistical data
- Price list of competitors
- Anything not commonly known (Terms, phrases, etc)

This is a sample of the sections of a business plan. There may be more or fewer topics, depending on your company's needs. Some people add their resumes. It shows they have the experience needed to run and manage a business correctly. There are loads of books out there that can help you write a business plan. If the funds are available you can hire someone to write the business plan for you. Either way, a business plan is not only necessary but it is essential (at least in my opinion).

I would also like to add that the wording of your business plan should reflect who you are and the nature of your business. It should be communicated in a manner that pleases the reader. In short, it has to be written for the reader. Know the language of the reader. Use words that the reader will understand.

Example: If you are going to seek funding to start an I.T. company but your reader is a banker, then you need to use language bankers will understand. Also use the appendix to clear up any words or jargon that may be specific to your industry and not commonly known.

Micro Lenders

Micro-lenders sometimes work in conjunction with banks. Often if a bank considers you too risky for a loan, and it is not worth it for them to send you to the SBA, they may have a relationship with a micro-lender. Micro-lenders have different lending criteria than a bank. They tend to work with smaller amounts that may range anywhere from 1000 to 50K. It really depends on the micro-lender. Micro-lenders tend to charge more interest than a bank. Their rationale is the higher the risk, the higher the interest charged. But that is true with all creditors. This fact should not deter you from using a micro-lender. They may assist you in opening the doors of your business.

One of the more popular micro lenders in the New York metropolitan area is Accion.

Venture Capitalist (VC's)

A venture capitalist is an investor that invests money into a start-up and expects a positive return for their investment. Since start-ups are extremely risky VC's usually want a big piece of the profit. They may ask for the controlling shares or decision making authority. Sometimes a VC will replace your management team with their own. A VC may be able to take your company to the open market faster.

VC's specialize in specific industries so you don't want to go to a VC that specializes in aviation if you have come up with a new car. If you do, then you may find yourself extremely aggravated and frustrated. You can look on the internet or read books for more detailed information.

At the end of the day if you have a vision along with passion, a good idea, stamina, and the balls to start your own business, it should not matter how you fund it. If that means you have to work another job until your business takes off, so be it. If that means you have to borrow money, then so be it. What is the worst thing that can happen? Remember the difference between you and other people is that you are an entrepreneur and entrepreneurs are risk takers.

Ideas/Notes

Staffing Your Business

The rise and fall of your business
depends on your leadership

-Anonymous-

STAFFING YOUR BUSINESS:

You have your business plan. You have your funding. Everything is in place. Now it's time to hire your staff. This section explores how to hire your staff - who to hire, when to hire them, and how to evaluate. Unfortunately you will have to fire someone at some time. So, this chapter also covers how to fire and when to do it.

6

Later in the chapter I discuss how to inspire and lead your team. All of this is necessary to make your business a success. If you cannot inspire and lead, you will find yourself constantly frustrated and aggravated. That is not a place for anyone to be, let alone an entrepreneur. Remember your business will rise and fall on the decisions you make as the leader.

The importance of hiring the correct people

The staff you hire is a reflection of you, your business, and what the two represent. You need to hire the right people. That person may not be the most experienced. They may not be the best at what they do. They don't have to be people you like personally. Yet they must represent your business and embrace the mission of your business.

Some of you reading this will say, if I hire them, I have to like them. My question to you is, "What if you need a sales person to complete your team?" The person that walks through the door has the credentials and desire, and can take your business to new heights. Why wouldn't "you" hire that person if he/she is the best person for the job? This may be the person that will enable you to achieve your goals. My suggestion is to put your personal differences aside, get to work, and make it happen.

Hiring your staff

When thinking about hiring, it is important to make a couple of quick assessments. You will need to identify critical work, required skills, and your ability to attract and pay. Now, to be certain if you are running a small enterprise, you may be tempted to limit your assessment to answering the question, "Where can I get the most bang for my buck?" I would caution you to avoid this mistake. It is just as important to hire the right person with skills for the present and future growth potential and a desire to succeed. When making your first hire it is like making your 100th hire. The point is in a small business that first hire may help make or break the business.

Every small business should follow the local, state, and federal labor laws as well as any additional rules and regulations that are applicable. This may mean a conversation with an attorney specializing in employment law. Well it is never too early to start building relationships with professionals whose services you may need in the future. If you do not know a reputable attorney, contact your state bar association for a referral. And know that many attorneys will provide basic guidance on a pro bono (yes, that is free) basis. As your business grows and you are able to pay, you may be able to turn to that same attorney as your company's external counsel. Just a quick reminder - you may have someone in your support group that works in HR that may also be able to assist you.

The internet is always available (I suggest using government sites) as a quick reference tool, but be careful of relying too heavily on information from internet sites. Many laws are very stable. However, the current focus on Homeland Security, immigration, and other areas that may affect employment may have caused changes in employment laws and practice. In short, you cannot do what a friend or relative did years ago. You should rely on direct counsel from a professional.

Who to hire

John C. Maxwell stated, "When you can't afford to hire the best, hire the young who are going to be the best." I agree this is a good practice. Entrepreneurs are often short on cash to hire the best. This means you have to hire the next best thing, who, according to John C. Maxwell, is the young who are going to be the best. The rationale behind it is that you can mold the young into what you need them to be. The young have a lot of assets. They are young for one. They have tons of energy. They are hungry. They feel as though they have to prove their worth so they sometimes work harder than their more seasoned counterparts.

Sometimes as an entrepreneur you will not have the funds available to hire needed staff. You may have to enlist the assistance of the people in your support group. My suggestion is that if you have to go that route, make sure the person shares your vision. And, at all costs you should pay them something. If this means you help them paint their house or baby sit, then that is what you do. Then it is less likely that hard feelings will occur. If your children work for you, make sure they understand you appreciate their help and maybe let them stay up a little later. You don't want to set the example of always getting something for nothing. Something else that may work is letting your child know (only if it's true), that you are planning to leave the business to them and you are not only doing this for yourself, but you're doing this for them as well.

In short, whoever you get to help, if they are not doing it for pay, you have to give them incentive. And show your gratitude for their help. Remember gratitude will get you far.

How much do you pay them?

The first thing you have to understand is not everyone is after money. There are people out there who will try to convince you that the key to obtaining good, quality staff is money. That's crap. And there are those that will say that you get what you pay for. When people say that, especially in regards to prospective employees, they are not considering the fact that money does not buy happiness, but it does rent it for a while. It buys comfort. With that said, for the best, you will have to compensate them with more than money. You will have to provide a custom package that only you can provide. That package must include great leadership and direction, potential for growth. You will have to provide an atmosphere that is caring, empowering, and full of trust. This, coupled with a fair amount of money, will make the best employees happy and will foster loyalty.

Dispel the notion that money is the sole determinant prospective employees want. If money is everything, why do people leave high paying jobs to explore more fulfilling jobs like teaching? Some people desire an opportunity for growth; some want safety; some want something challenging to do; some want excitement. There are those that want it all. Your challenge is to figure out what type of person you need.

In order to attract good quality employees for your business, you have to care about your business and the people. There are various web sites you can go to, to get an estimate of what fair market value is for your needs (e.g. www.salary.com)

Face it, we can no longer just throw money at people, we have to provide quality of life with quality of work.

How should you evaluate your team?

Before evaluating your team, take a self evaluation to measure your own performance in their eyes. Ask yourself the following questions: Do I lead with passion, confidence, and a desire to help others. Do I communicate my thoughts well? How well do I listen to my team? Is there an open line of communication? The previous questions are few in number and are just the tip of the iceberg before you begin evaluating your team. When your evaluation is accurate and honest, then begin your team's evaluation. You can use the same criteria to evaluate yourself, as you do for your team.

How do you motivate your team?

First thing is first; you have to understand a few things in motivating others. I will begin by saying your team has to believe you are in the trenches with them. Second, motivation begins with you. Third, you have to provide an atmosphere of safety, passion, and open communication. You cannot motivate anyone. This is so important it needs to be repeated: you cannot motivate anyone. They must want to be motivated. Your team will tell you how to motivate them in actions. They will respond to your actions by wanting to please you and do what's best for the business. Yes, you will find some who you will not have to motivate as much as others, but again, everything hinges on you. You will have to find the best methods to work with your team. It all starts with your ability to communicate, listen, look, and take action.

How do you fire someone on your team?

Firing a team member may be the hardest thing a leader has to do. Firing a team member is the last thing you want to do. You may feel guilty for firing a person you have built a relationship with because you know it may hurt them in more ways than one. The firing may be a reflection of your inability to lead or a lack of proper communication on your part. But you have to remember you have to do what's best for the whole team and for your business. Your company is only as strong as its weakest link.

Before you ever get to the point when you have to fire a team member, you should have had several conversations trying to figure out what went wrong. As the leader, that is your job. As a precaution, you should document all conversations and track agreements.

How to manage your team?

Going back to the root - you; if you cannot manage yourself, you cannot manage others. In other words, management begins and ends with the way you manage yourself. The comedian Chris Rock was talking about relationships and how people aren't themselves. They bring their representatives. Then months later you find the real person. This is the case with hiring and managing people. The person you hired is not always what they are cracked up to be and the person you hire must fit the culture of the company.

Often, the person you interviewed is not the person that currently works for you. One day you could come into work and look at your employee and say to yourself, "How in the hell did this happen?" Kind of like the night you had one too many and woke up next to the wrong person.

Conversely, you may court the person and entice them to work for you. Then months later the employee doesn't see the person who hired them. They see the real you. Make sure you are always true to yourself and others.

Always be yourself no matter what. Then your employees will know what they are getting into before they start.

Ideas/Notes

Maintaining Your Business

Obstacles are those frightful things you
see when you take your eyes off your goal

-Henry Ford-

MAINTAINING YOUR BUSINESS:

Maintaining Your Business

Maintaining your business involves several things: staying true to your mission; maintaining your vision; adapting to change quickly; and keeping your eyes on the prize. You must stay in the present with your eye on the future. That means you must be willing to change.

A lot of businesses fail because the owner loses focus. Sometimes it's because they just aren't sure how to manage and maintain the day-to-day business activities. Other times, they lose their passion for the business or found the creation process more enticing. There are many reasons why a business may lose momentum. This chapter will assist you in maintaining your business.

Preserving the mission and goal of your business is essential to maintaining your business. This is not to suggest you should resist change. You always have to be prepared for change. Just keep your original mission in mind. Dealing with change can be difficult, but you should embrace change and look at it as an opportunity. If you need help seeing when to change or the benefit of change, read the book "Who Moved My Cheese." It is one of the best books around that deals with change and can be applied to your life, business, spiritual or personal change.

If the mission of your business is providing excellent customer service, then that excellent customer service begins with you the owner. Secondly, it must be maintained by you. Third, show gratitude. A smile saying thank you and being grateful will not cost you anything, but not doing may cost you your business.

Not too long ago I had a friend who opened a boutique that sold very fine clothing. The boutique was a little expensive but he was doing very well. He had the best customer service ever and that was the main reason his customers continued to shop there. Several months after the opening, I went into the store and found it empty. I called my friend and ask him what was going on with his business. He did not have a clue. I asked him what he had done to retain his clientele and his response was that he had reduced the cost of the clothing. He stayed open a little longer and was stocked with the newest and hottest clothing, but his customers "disappeared" on him. To my surprise he asked me for my assistance. I of course agreed.

I went into the store and the workers treated me like gold. They were very attentive. I could not figure out what the issue was. I began to take a mental inventory and all seemed to be in place. I began talking to another friend and he told me that he was reading the Art of War and I remembered that Sun Tzu believed in knowing ones' enemy as well as oneself.

I enlisted the help of some friends to be mystery shoppers at the boutique and at similar stores in the area. To my surprise the boutique's employees were rude and non attentive. So the former patrons of the store were chased away. I reported my findings to my friend and he was shocked.

After speaking to the employees, I found that because my friend ignored them, they in turn ignored the customers. This reminded me of the book "The Tipping Point." In The Tipping Point, there was a part that talked about the broken window theory which in this instance means the owner did not care about the employees so they did not care about the customers.

Remember, in business you have to pay attention to your customers, and everyone is your customer. Your customers are more than the people purchasing your products or services. They are anyone you have to provide a service to, including your employees. No matter how big your company, customer service begins at the top and it is passed down through the employees to the customers. In short, shit rolls downhill.

Integrity

If you sacrifice your personal integrity, your business will suffer and worse than your business suffering, your spirit will suffer.

Success! Now what?

Whatever your success is, whatever you have defined your success to be, whether it is to have several locations, or a particular dollar amount, you need to keep your mind on the future. What do you do now? My suggestion is to give back. Yes, give back to the communities that helped you obtain your success. Give in a way that adds value to the community and helps it thrive.

By donating computers to inner city schools, Dell promotes its products, builds a future customer base, and helps students in the education process. You should consider donating your time, experience, and knowledge providing internships or sponsoring a school's sports team.

I have heard excuses for not giving back. For example, I don't have the time. I have not made it so how can I help others make it. Remember excuses are like assholes; everyone has them and they all STINK.

Staying motivated

Staying motivated can be extremely hard. Sometimes life gets in the way - family, responsibilities, and most of all, you. You may even find it very difficult to get out of bed some mornings. First, know that everyone has those days; the difference between you being a winner and a lot of other people is that you get up and take action. No progress can occur without action.

Techniques to stay motivated

Depending on how de-motivated I feel or why I feel de-motivated dictates what course of action I will take. The first course of action I would take is to identify the cause of my de-motivation. If I find that I am tired because I have been grinding hard and long, I schedule break time in my calendar. We all need to rest and sometimes we forget to recharge. There are those times when I feel like everything has become routine. So I change it up a little bit. It may just be what time I begin work or changing the time I go to the gym. Sometimes I spend time doing something else. There are other things to do, for example, re-read my personal mission.

Adapting to change

A huge part of maintaining your business is being able to recognize new trends and adapting to them. If you are unwilling or unable to adapt to change, you may lose time and money. The world is becoming smaller and smaller because of the internet. There are other changes you should prepare for other than the cyber world. There are local changes, economic changes, changes in trends, styles and even the way business is conducted. As an entrepreneur it is your job to be a visionary - spot the changes. Develop a strategy, and make a profit. The following are some ways to identify changes around you and ways to adapt to change.

Indicators
1. Your business begins to slow down.
2. Your team doesn't have anything to do.
3. Your business begins to stagnate.
4. Losing money
5. Paying your team with your credit cards.
6. You have lost your focus.

Ways to adapt to change

1. Recognize something is going on and take action.
2. Subscribe to and read periodicals and magazines.
3. Join a local city economic development center.
4. Walk around your neighborhood and notice any changes.
5. Talk to other business owners. They may have gone through what you are going through.

Ideas/Notes

Ideas/Notes

Ways to Lead Your Business To Victory

Action is the foundational key to all success
-Pablo Picasso-

WAYS TO LEAD YOUR TEAM TO VICTORY:

Leaders have passion, commitment, influence, integrity and a willingness to learn. There is one more important quality a leader must have - a leader must love people. If you do not love people then how are you going to lead them? Another question, where are you going to lead? I am sure you have some, if not all of those qualities. The following is a small leadership test. This test will show some indication of whether you will be a good leader or if you need some leadership training.

Leadership test

Questions	Yes	No
Do you love people?		
Do you inspire people?		
Do you value the opinion of others?		
Do you lead by example?		
Are you committed to the development of others?		
Are you passionate?		

If you have more "yes" than "no" responses, then you are on the right track. If you have more "no's" than "yes" there is still hope; you may need to develop your leadership skills.

How to lead your team to victory

When you lead without your heart, you will think of yourself first. When you lead without using your gut feeling, you will never develop confidence in yourself and the people you are leading will never develop confidence in your leadership. If you lead devoid of clarity of mind, you will not make the right choices. If you lead without having the facts, your leadership will always be questioned.

I started this chapter this way because these are things you should consider before making a decision. Gather the facts - lead with all of the information available to you. This is not only important but it is essential. There is little chance you can make an informed decision without being informed. If you think of yourself first and not the people, you are not leading; these people will lose respect for you because you do not take their needs into account. There are some decisions you will make that require the use of both your heart and your mind. You may have to rely more heavily on your gut feeling. If you don't trust your gut, you will undoubtedly second guess yourself and make a mistake.

One of the best ways I know how to lead is by example. If you have a person who is cleaning, get down and clean with them. That will show your employees you are willing to get dirty and are able to experience things from their perspective. Owners may lose touch with what it's like to be in the trenches; so talk to your employees, find out what is going on, and what issues they are facing. Make sure you don't solve all of the issues for them, rather assist them in solving the issues for themselves. If you solve the issues for them, you will create a dependence on you to think for them. Empower your employees to make decisions within their realm of expertise.

Imagine you are the owner of a gym. One of your employees has been working out for years and has years of experience as a fitness trainer. Perhaps you could let that person recommend your next piece of fitness equipment. If you do, you have just empowered that employee and you will have time to do something else. That is a small example of leadership. There are many books on leadership that can teach you in some respects, but you have to take action and learn in the trenches.

The importance leadership plays in business

Businesses rise and fall on how well the leader or owner plays their role. Wars are won by soldiers and lost by the generals. To put in no uncertain terms, leadership loses the battle. You can have the best idea, concept, and business plan, but without the proper leadership, chances are you will never realize the fruits of your labor.

Believing in your vision

There aren't many ways to put this, so I will just put it out there for you. It's quite simple - if you don't believe whole heartedly in your vision, how in the hell can you get someone else to believe your vision? For that matter, why should they? I mentioned this earlier in the book because of its importance. I cannot stress it enough. You have to believe in yourself and part of it is to believe in your vision. I can't tell you how many projects I have worked on or how many jobs I have had where I did not believe in myself. As a result, I second guessed myself; I became fearful and did not act or just quit. It has taken me a long time to get over that issue. Enough said. Believe and you can achieve.

Believing in yourself

One of the reasons why we may not believe in ourselves is because we don't know how. We have experienced setbacks which turned into failures.

I have three children who have taught me a lot. I learned that even if you fall and get scraped up, you can get up and continue. One day, I had taken my sons to the park and my son, Robert, was playing on the jungle gym. He saw some older children climbing up this metal rope ladder. So Robert being the daring child he is tried it and fell pretty hard. He cried. I was not certain whether he was crying because he fell and was hurt, or because he did not make it up the ladder. The next day he tried the ladder and fell again. Later on that same day, he attempted it again and this time I made him stop for fear he would get hurt. The third day, while tying my other son's sneaker, Robert started on his way to the ladder. Before I knew it, he went up the ladder and finally my baby made it. I was so proud of him, not because he made it up the ladder, but because he did not give up. My son, two at the time, taught me a valuable lesson. In my opinion, Robert believed in his ability to get up that ladder. Even if he experienced a setback, he did not let that hold him back.

There are a lot of people out there who believe in themselves. There are people out there who face insurmountable odds and beat them. One day I was in the gym working out and I starting feeling like I was in a rut. I started complaining, which is never good because it's a waste of energy - I complained about the music; I complained about work; I complained that I was feeling old because of the aches and pains I felt.

An older man walked in and I noticed him limping. I took a closer look and noticed he had a prosthetic leg. But he looked great. He wasn't the most buffed person there nor was he the youngest, but there was something about him. He got on the treadmill and began running. About an hour later when I finished my work out he was still running. After my shower and getting a protein drink I noticed that he was still running and at an even faster pace than when he started. I thought wow this guy is an inspiration. He was like that energizer rabbit that keeps going and going.

He finally stopped running and came over to the counter where I was drinking my protein shake. I began a conversation with him by asking, "Are you training for anything?" His reply was, "Yes, the New York Marathon." I guess he saw the amazement in my eyes and then he said, "It's my fourth one. I am trying to beat my time last year." To which I asked, "Does your leg bother you?" He replied, "Yeah my knee is starting to hurt," and laughed it off.

We became gym friends. He would give me advice on running and I in turn would give him advice on weight training. During that time, I finally felt comfortable enough and asked him how he lost his leg. He told me that his leg was crushed in a car accident. I asked him how he felt about losing his leg and he responded, "It's gone so I have to go on." I asked if he ever doubted whether he would run again and he said, "Nope, nothing can stop me from running even if I lost my other leg. I would still run, maybe even faster than I do now."

I don't remember his name but his story always sticks with me. He did not give up and he believed in himself. My gym friend was an inspiration to me and probably to many other people that knew him. He believed. There are many more stories out there where people have beaten the odds. Use one that touches you. Remember, if you believe, you can achieve.

Believing in your team

Your team is an extension of you and if you don't believe in your team, you don't believe in yourself. If you have hired them, I am confident that you have chosen the best people for the job. Teamwork makes the dream work. Remember that leading your team to victory is a constant challenge even for the most seasoned leader. And even those leaders did not lead their teams to victory all of the time. Take a look at professional sports teams such as The New York Yankees. Remember when the Boston Red Sox beat the Yankees in the World Series? On paper the Yankees were a much better team player (the most expensive), better coaching, and just better overall. Then you have the Boston Red Sox, a team that won a lot of games in the same year. They were strong with good players and a good coach, but were they stellar? Could they compare to the Yankees? They had fight, heart, desire and belief. They were in it to win it. The players believed, the coach believed, and their fans believed. We all know the outcome. The Yankees lost. Sometimes, those who believe in themselves the most make the difference in the outcome.

People always feel special and are willing to work a little harder and a little longer for a person that believes in them. They never want to disappoint the person/leader that believes in them.

Take a look at your parents, people who really believed in you. Remember when they were disappointed in something you did and the look on their faces and how did that make you feel? The next time you tried even harder. I am sure you can remember that. Well, a lot of the times that is how your employees will look at you.

Motivating others by action

People tend to respect the person, not the position. In motivating others, you have to be willing to get your hands dirty. Earlier in this book I mentioned leading by example. That still stands true. One of the best ways to motivate a person is to work with them, not against them. Find out what makes them tick, what makes them happy, and help them achieve it. Allow them to do the same for you. If you can help them and allow them to help you, they will feel empowered. Giving the feeling of empowerment to someone motivates them to new heights.

Being respected for the person you are not for the position you hold

As an entrepreneur, leader, or manager, you hold a great power and because of that you have a great responsibility. In the movie Spiderman, Peter Parker was talking to his uncle Ben who said, "With great power comes great responsibility." You have the power to change lives by giving them a job; by being their support; by empowering them. The way you receive respect is to give respect. In the previous section, motivating others by action is a part of obtaining respect. There is another important aspect which is caring about your fellow man. Not for what you can get out of it, but genuinely caring about their growth as a person; as an employee; or whatever they are and want to be. You have to care. Whether you are an entrepreneur, a leader, or a manager, you have great power and should use it responsibly.

What is the difference between a leader, a manager, and you?

I was reading a book and I am not sure of the title or the author. In the book it clearly states the difference between a manager and a leader. The author is most likely John C. Maxwell. He says "A manager gets a process done through people. A leader inspires people to go above and beyond the call of duty." There are lots of leaders out there and there have been great leaders - Malcolm X, J.F.K, Dr. Martin Luther King Jr., the pastor at your local church, loads of CEO's, your parents, and various others. You may not be on the list but you are a leader in your own right.

Leadership has to do with your ability to influence and inspire people - it's how you influence those people that make you a great leader. I'm sure you have influenced someone. It may have been a classmate, co-workers, or a child. We all have some influence over some people. We have all inspired someone.

How to inspire yourself

If you have never been there then you can't lead someone there. Get there in your mind; then get everyone else there as well. You can do it. You have vision, passion, clarity of mind, and spirit.

Sometimes inspiring yourself is harder than inspiring others and may require you to dig down deeper than you ever have before. It may require more strength than you think you have. Before I get into techniques, I want you to know you can dig down deeper than you have before and you have more strength than you know you have. There is a saying that says "God only gives you what you can handle." If you could not handle it, you would not have it.

There are several things I do to inspire myself - I read a lot and may even reread a book I like. Spending time with my family and friends and talking to them about what's going on helps as well. If the feelings I have are very negative,

I write them down on paper and then ball up the paper and throw it away or burn it. I also remember all that I have gone through and how I am still standing and that helps me continue. Sometimes I go and help someone else out for no reason. I am sure you have things or events that have inspired you to greatness. Draw on your past experiences and set them to help you. What method you use rests on your shoulders.

Conclusion

I will leave you with this: Embrace your greatness and the greatness within you. Share your greatness with others selflessly. If you do this, you will be truly great. Also, if you want good things to happen, get up off of your ass and make good things happen.

Ideas/Notes

References

Spencer, Johnson M.D. "Who Moved My Cheese" New York.: G. P. Putman's Son, 1998.

Thomas Cleary "The art of War" Boston: Shambhala Publications, Inc. 1988.

John C. Maxwell "360 Degree Leader" Nashville: Thomas Nelson, 2006.

Russell Simons, Chris Marrow "Do you! New York: Gotham Books, 2007.

Malcolm Gladwell "The Tipping Point" Boston: Little, Brown and Company, 2000.